Rocks, baked in the heat
of an ancient sun,
line up straight as arrows
all across the desert floor
until finally merging with the mountain.

Copyright © 2023 Anita Jepson-Gilbert.

All rights reserved. No part of this book may be reproduced, stored, or transmitted by any means—whether auditory, graphic, mechanical, or electronic—without written permission of both publisher and author, except in the case of brief excerpts used in critical articles and reviews. Unauthorized reproduction of any part of this work is illegal and is punishable by law.

ISBN: 979-8-88640-621-4 (sc)
ISBN: 979-8-88640-622-1 (hc)
ISBN: 979-8-88640-623-8 (e)

Because of the dynamic nature of the Internet, any web addresses or links contained in this book may have changed since publication and may no longer be valid. The views expressed in this work are solely those of the author and do not necessarily reflect the views of the publisher, and the publisher hereby disclaims any responsibility for them.

One Galleria Blvd., Suite 1900, Metairie, LA 70001
1-888-421-2397

"Curious lines," thought the lady mathematician.
There were circles and triangles,
rectangles that could be highways,
quadrangles that looked like runways.

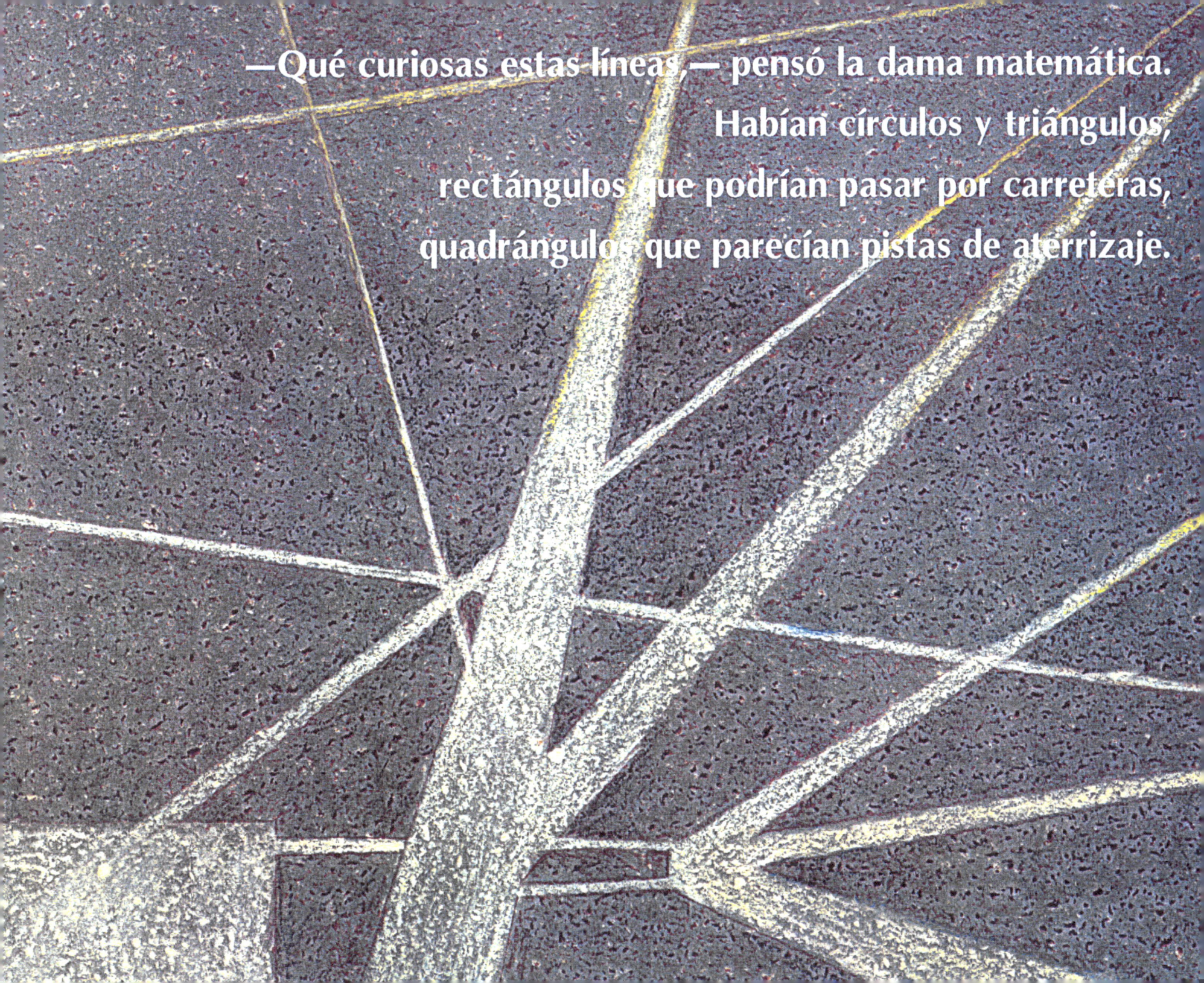

—Qué curiosas estas líneas,— pensó la dama matemática.
Habían círculos y triángulos,
rectángulos que podrían pasar por carreteras,
quadrángulos que parecían pistas de aterrizaje.

Lines she saw of every kind
crisscrossing north and east,
zigzagging south and west,
but leading nowhere.

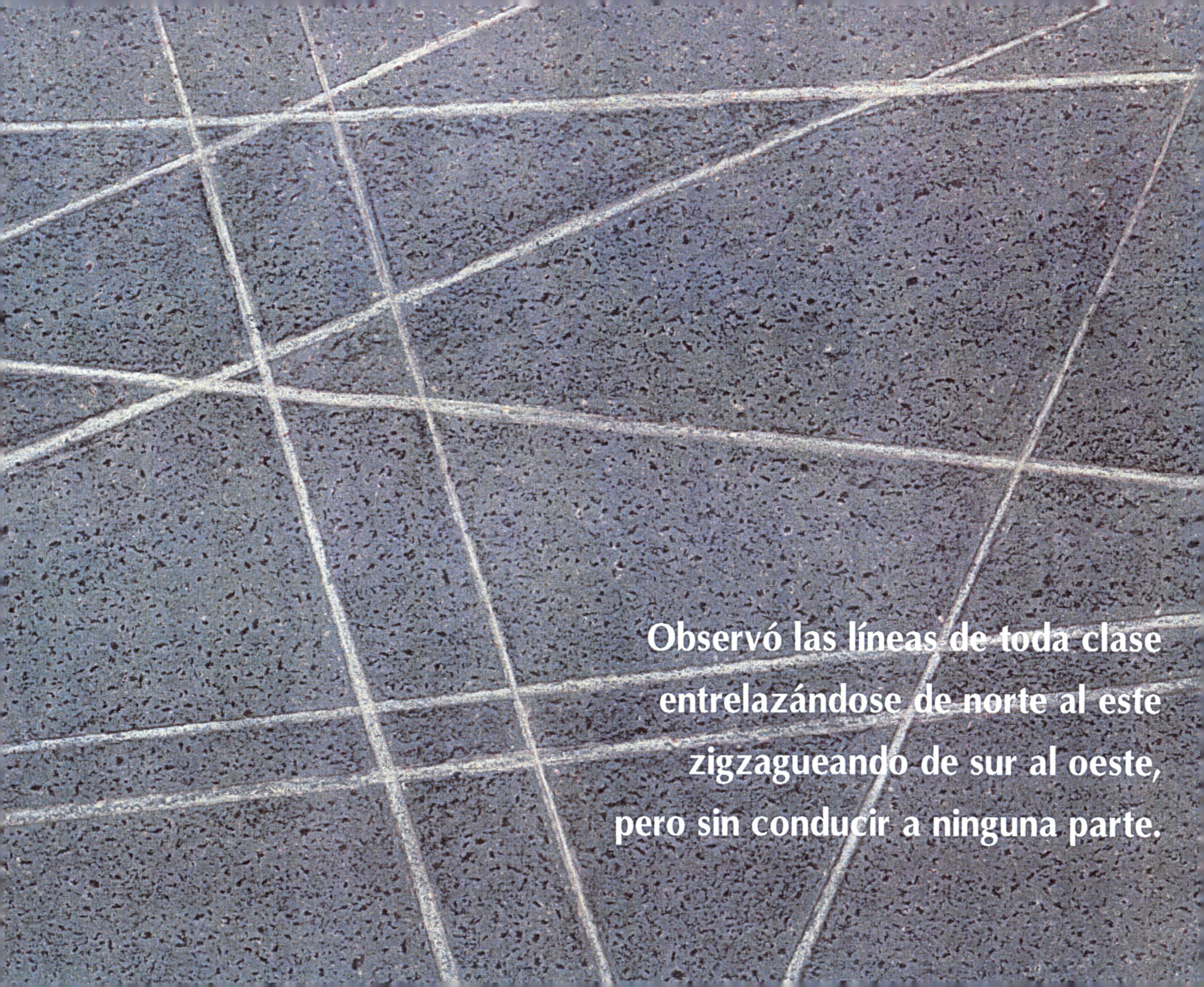

Observó las líneas de toda clase
entrelazándose de norte al este
zigzagueando de sur al oeste,
pero sin conducir a ninguna parte.

Entranced, Maria walked the lines,
her body from another land,
her spirit drawn to this desert sand
full of rocks and lines and mystery.

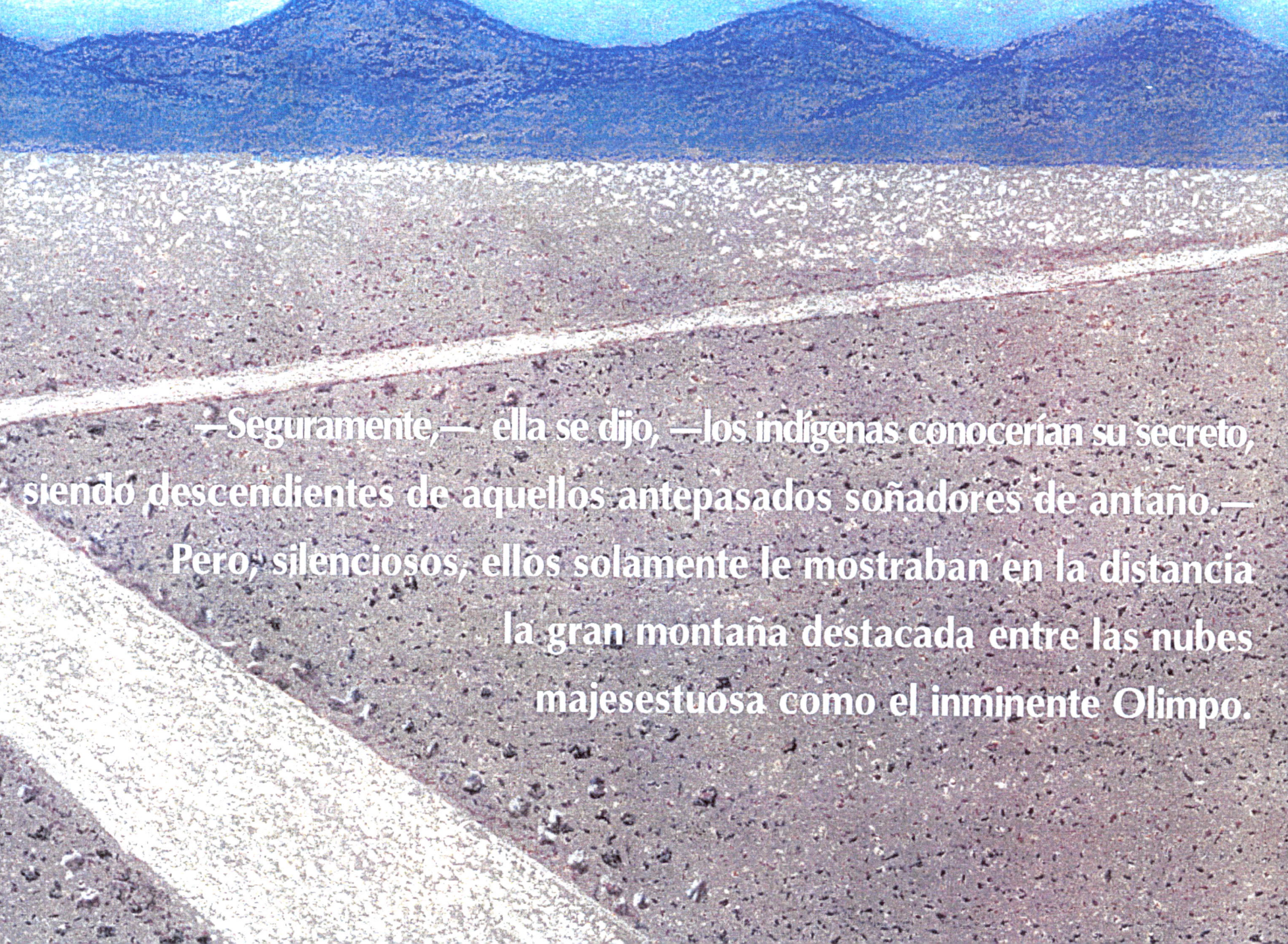

—Seguramente,— ella se dijo, —los indígenas conocerían su secreto, siendo descendientes de aquellos antepasados soñadores de antaño.— Pero, silenciosos, ellos solamente le mostraban en la distancia la gran montaña destacada entre las nubes majesestuosa como el inminente Olimpo.

She climbed until the vision cleared:
So many lines—some straight, some curved—
finally they revealed the true rulers
of Peru's ancestral ground.

María subió a la montaña hasta ver
con más claridad los dibujos tallados en el suelo:
Tantas líneas — unas rectas, otras torcidas, encorvadas—
finalmente revelaron los caciques gobernadores
de esta tierra ancestral peruana:

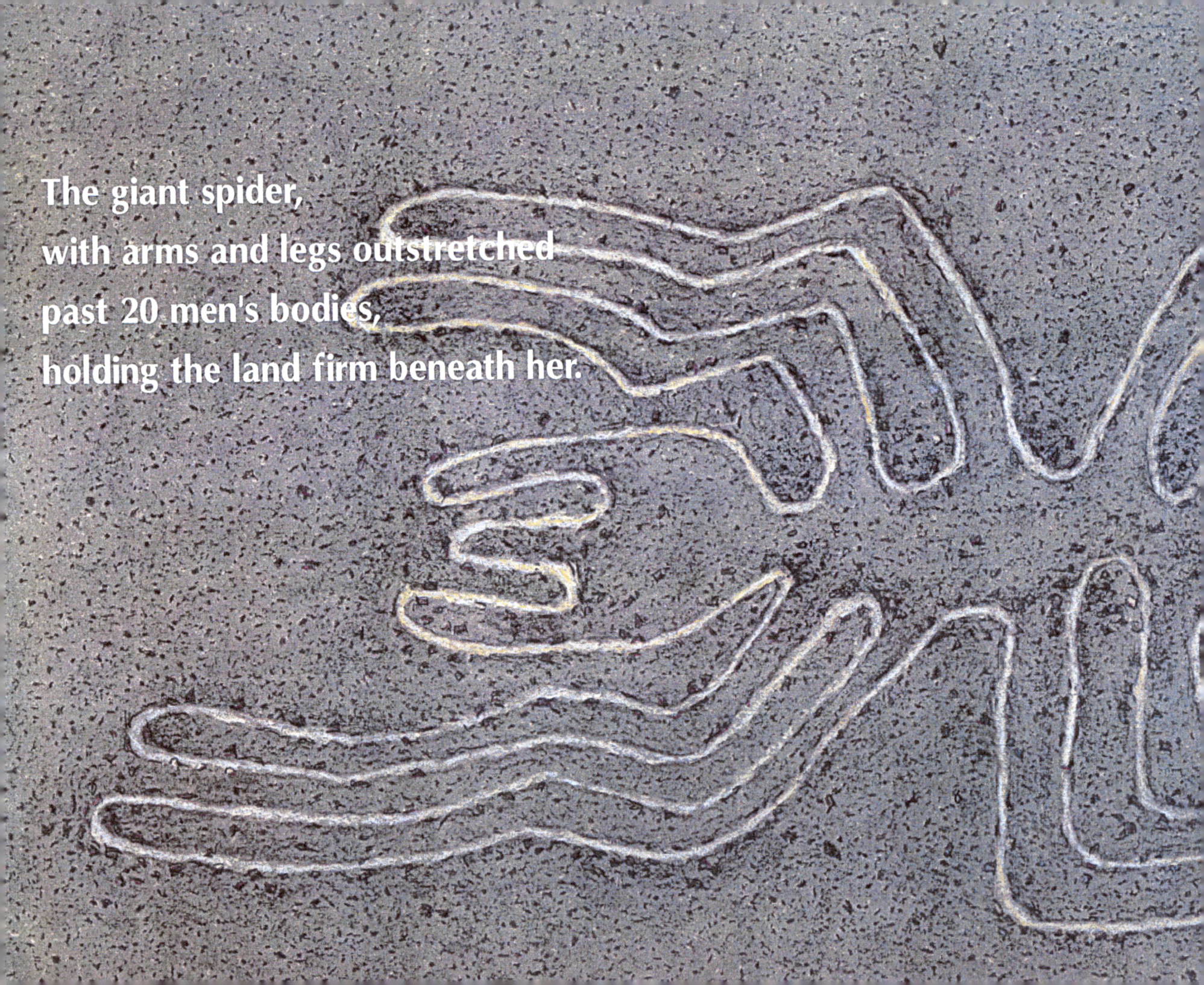

The giant spider,
with arms and legs outstretched
past 20 men's bodies,
holding the land firm beneath her.

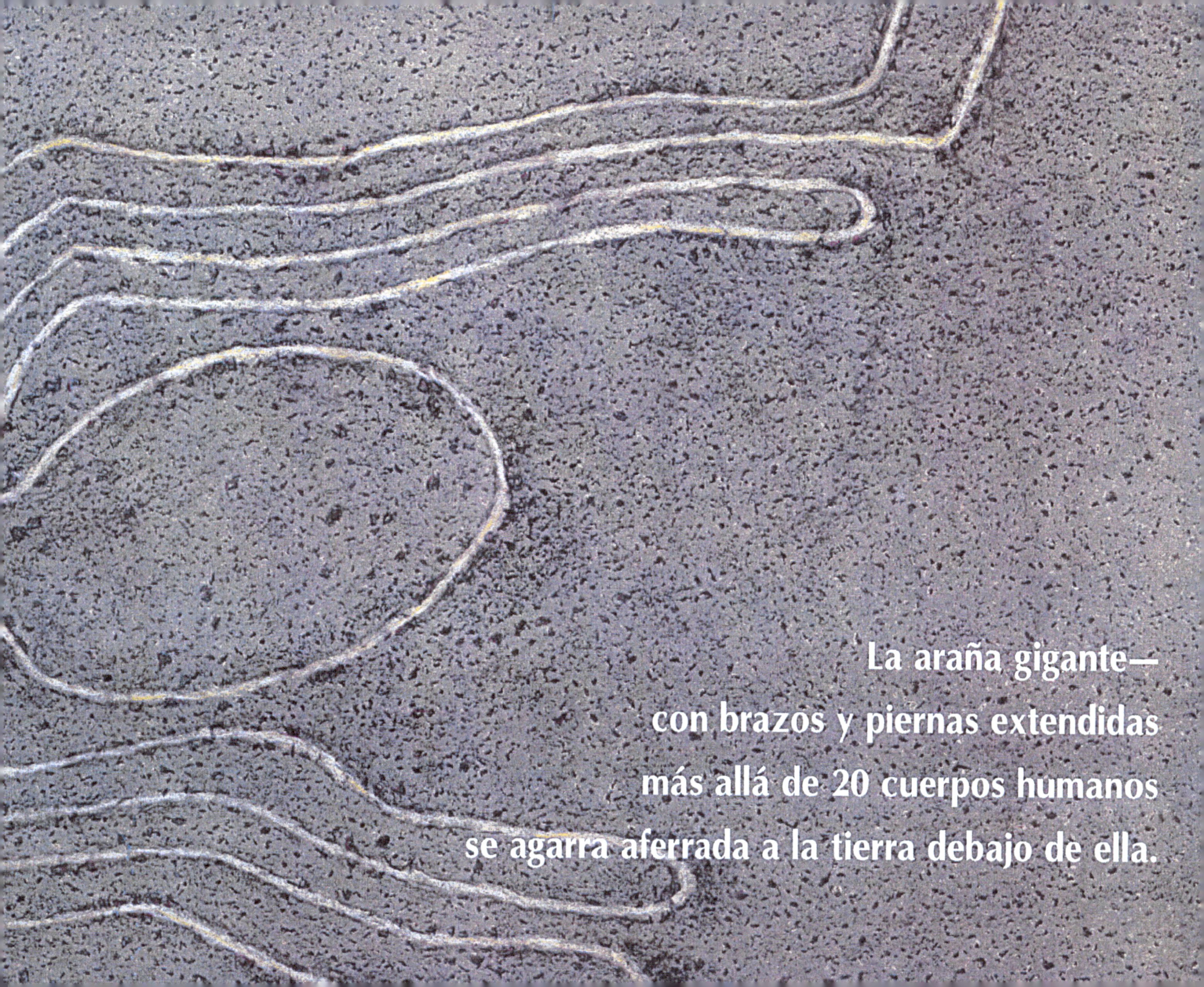

La araña gigante—
con brazos y piernas extendidas
más allá de 20 cuerpos humanos
se agarra aferrada a la tierra debajo de ella.

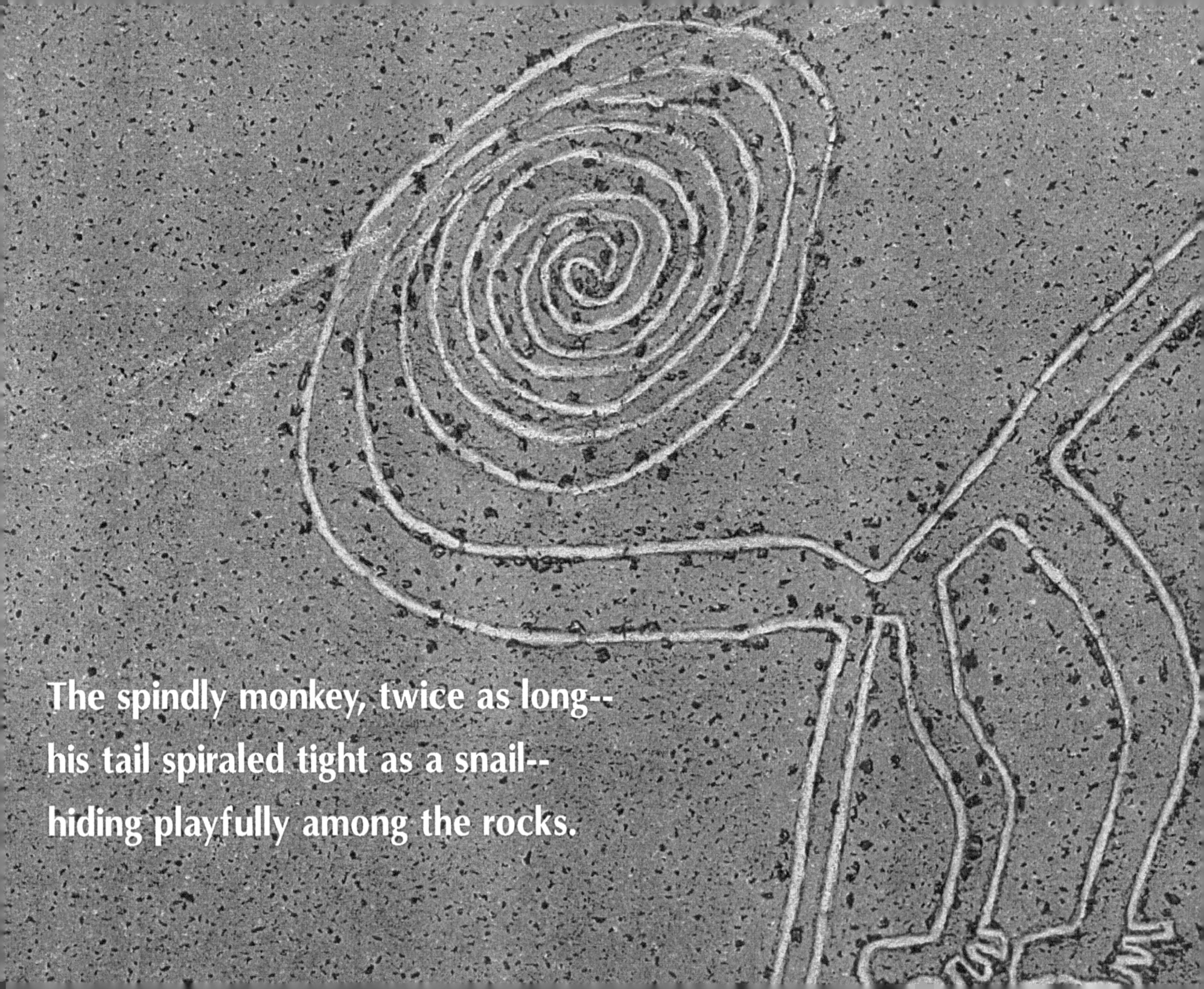

The spindly monkey, twice as long--
his tail spiraled tight as a snail--
hiding playfully among the rocks.

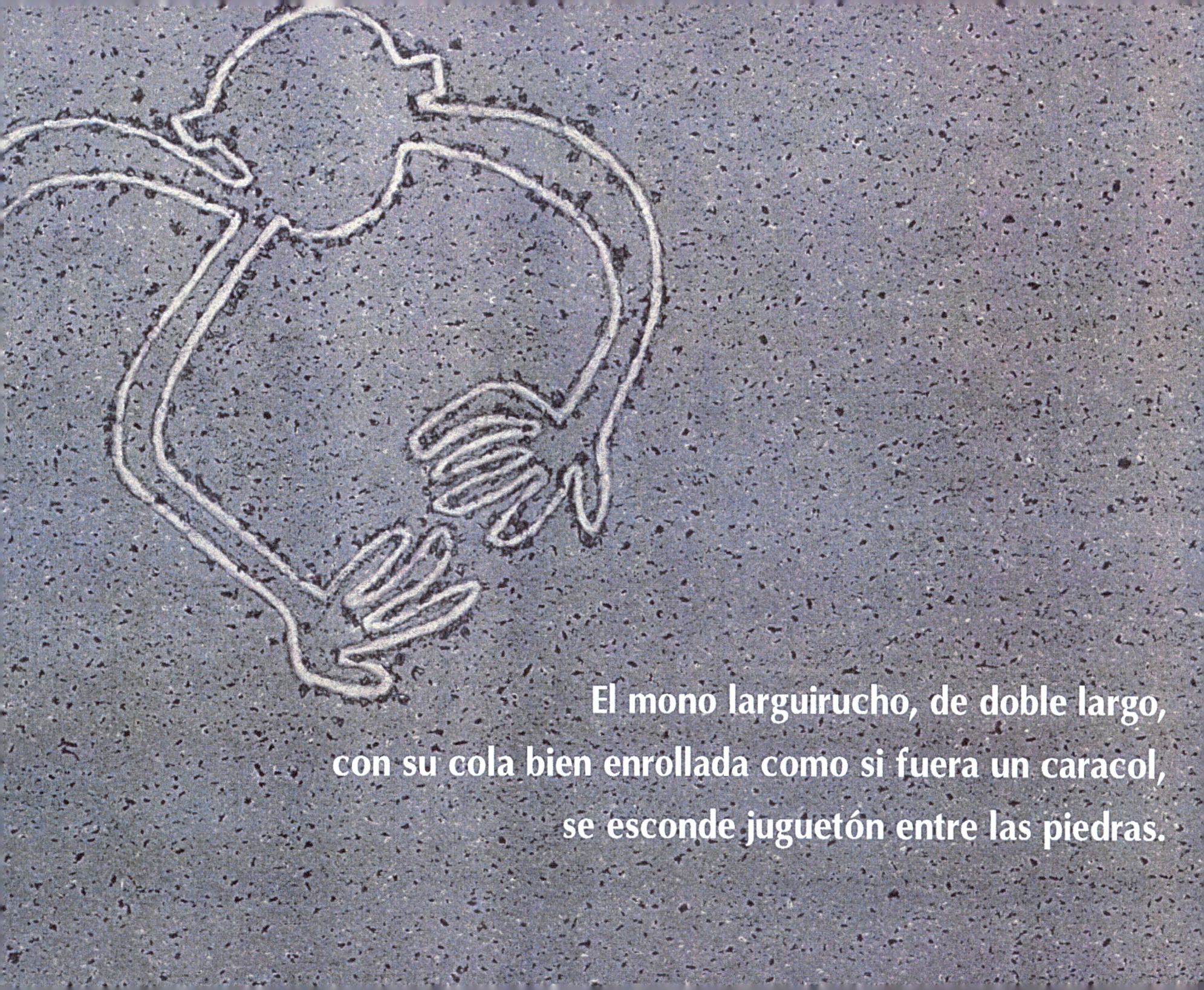

El mono larguirucho, de doble largo,
con su cola bien enrollada como si fuera un caracol,
se esconde juguetón entre las piedras.

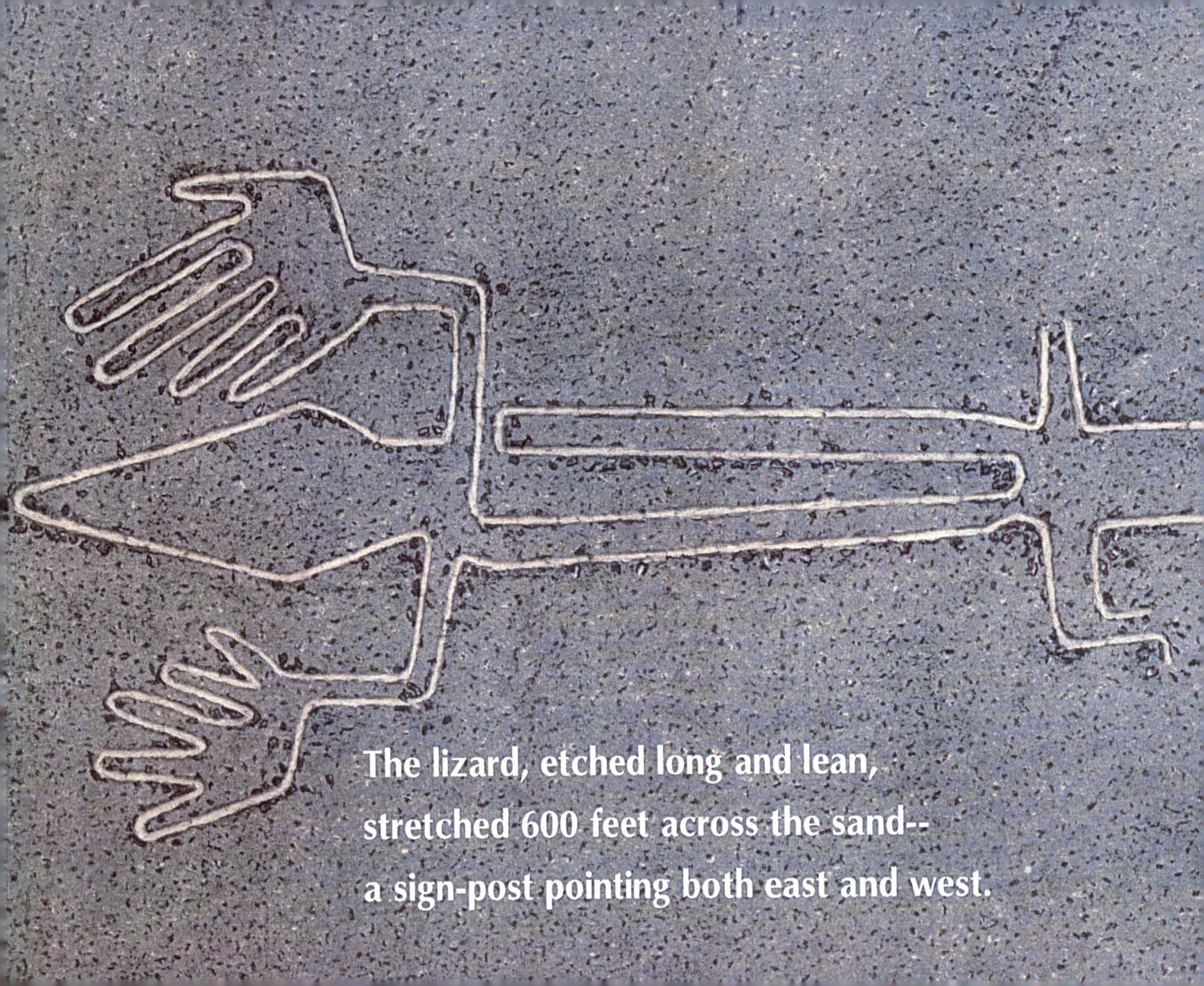

The lizard, etched long and lean,
stretched 600 feet across the sand--
a sign-post pointing both east and west.

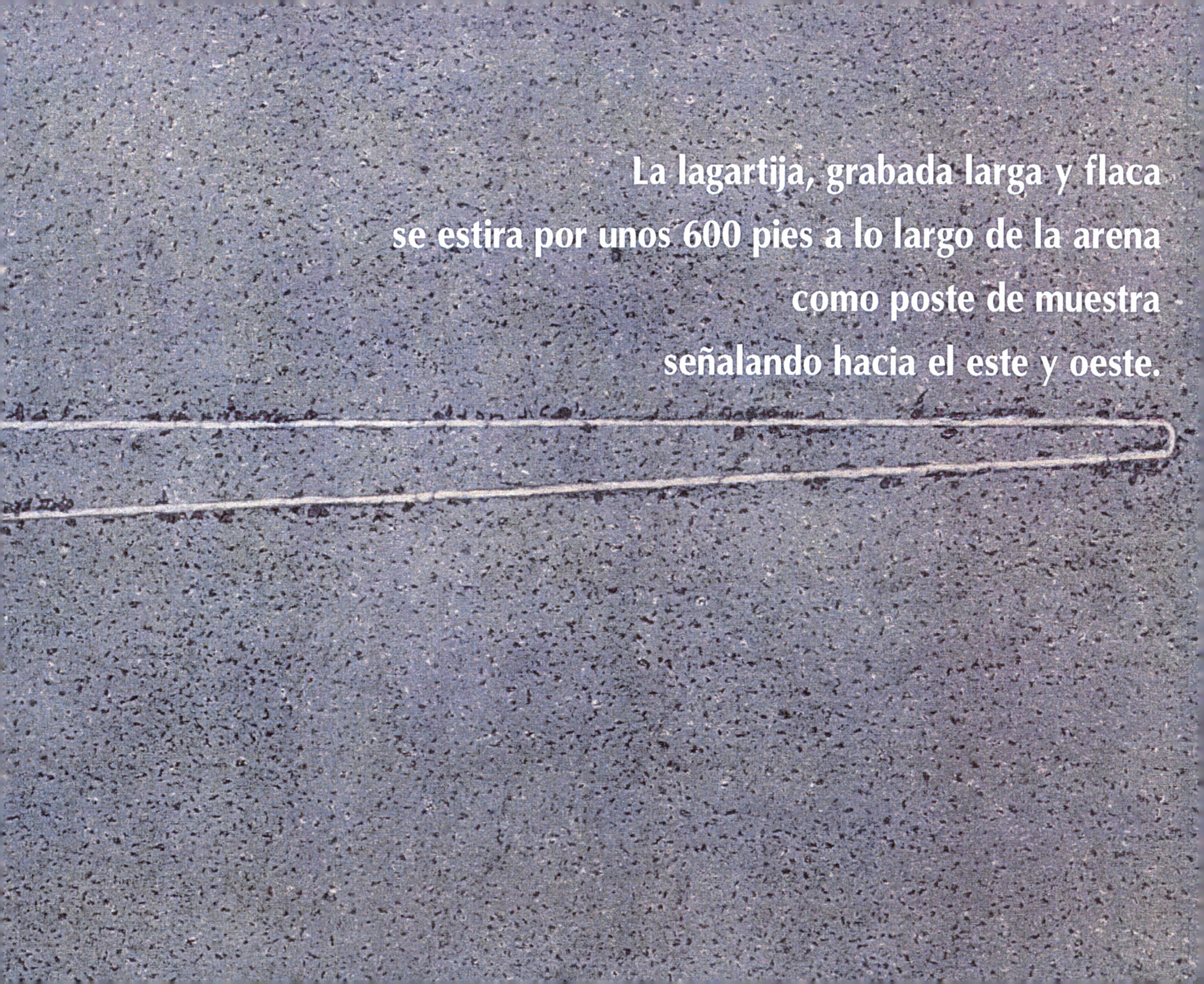

La lagartija, grabada larga y flaca
se estira por unos 600 pies a lo largo de la arena
como poste de muestra
señalando hacia el este y oeste.

A dog stands high on tiptoe
with his tail straight up in the air.
Perhaps he's seen the lizard
and is paralyzed with fear.

Un perro estirado de puntillas alzando en alto su trasero
con su cola apuntada recta en el aire,
quizás se da cuenta de la lagartija
y así se queda paralizado de miedo.

The iguana only laughs
at all the funny sights,
like the bird with a crooked neck,
who looks like he's swallowed a snake.

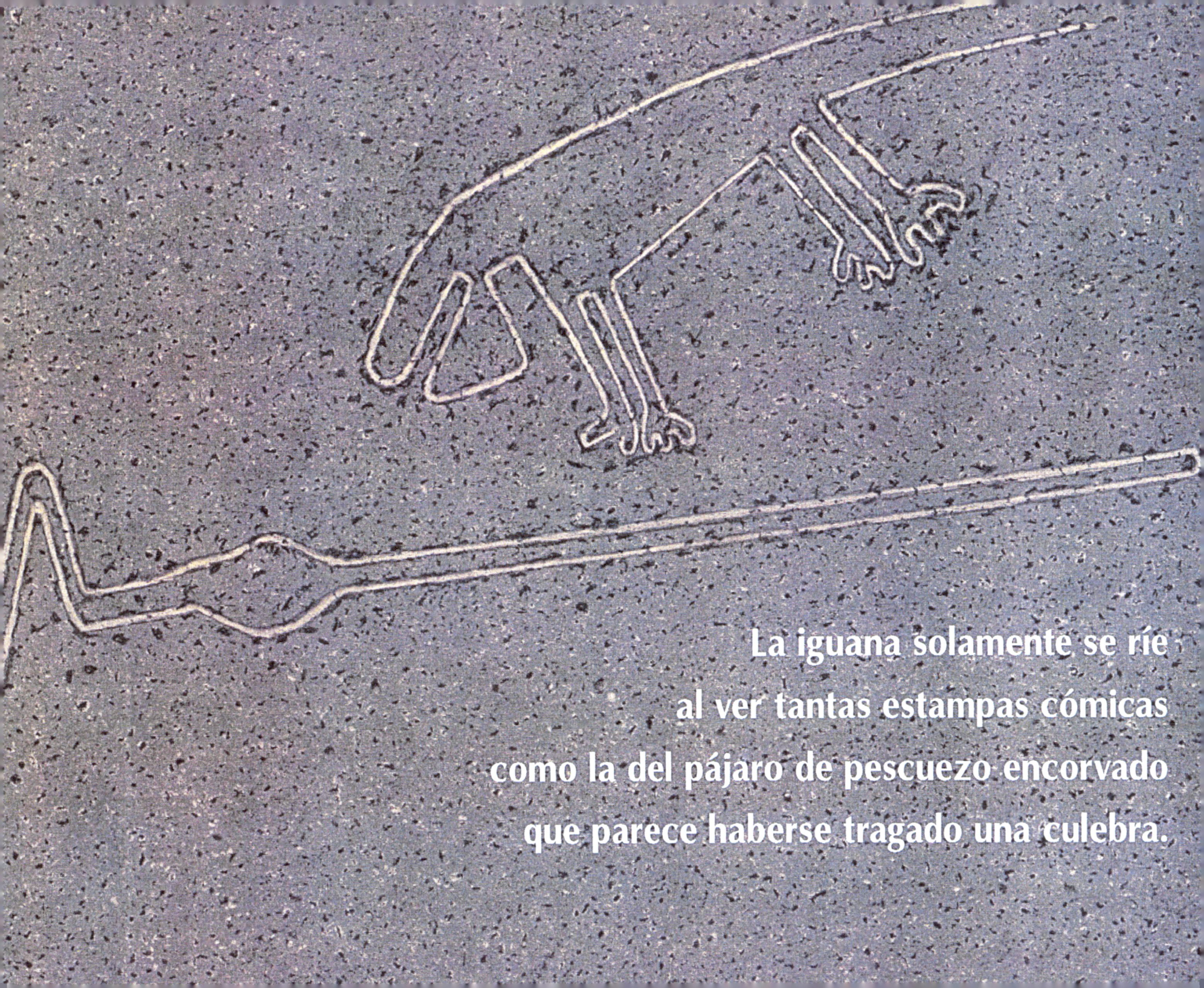

La iguana solamente se ríe
al ver tantas estampas cómicas
como la del pájaro de pescuezo encorvado
que parece haberse tragado una culebra.

The hummingbird--messenger from the gods--
his long beak piercing the ground.
What on earth could he have found?

El picaflor zumbidor—mensajero de los dioses—
con su pico largo enterrado bajo tierra.
¿Qué habrá encontrado?

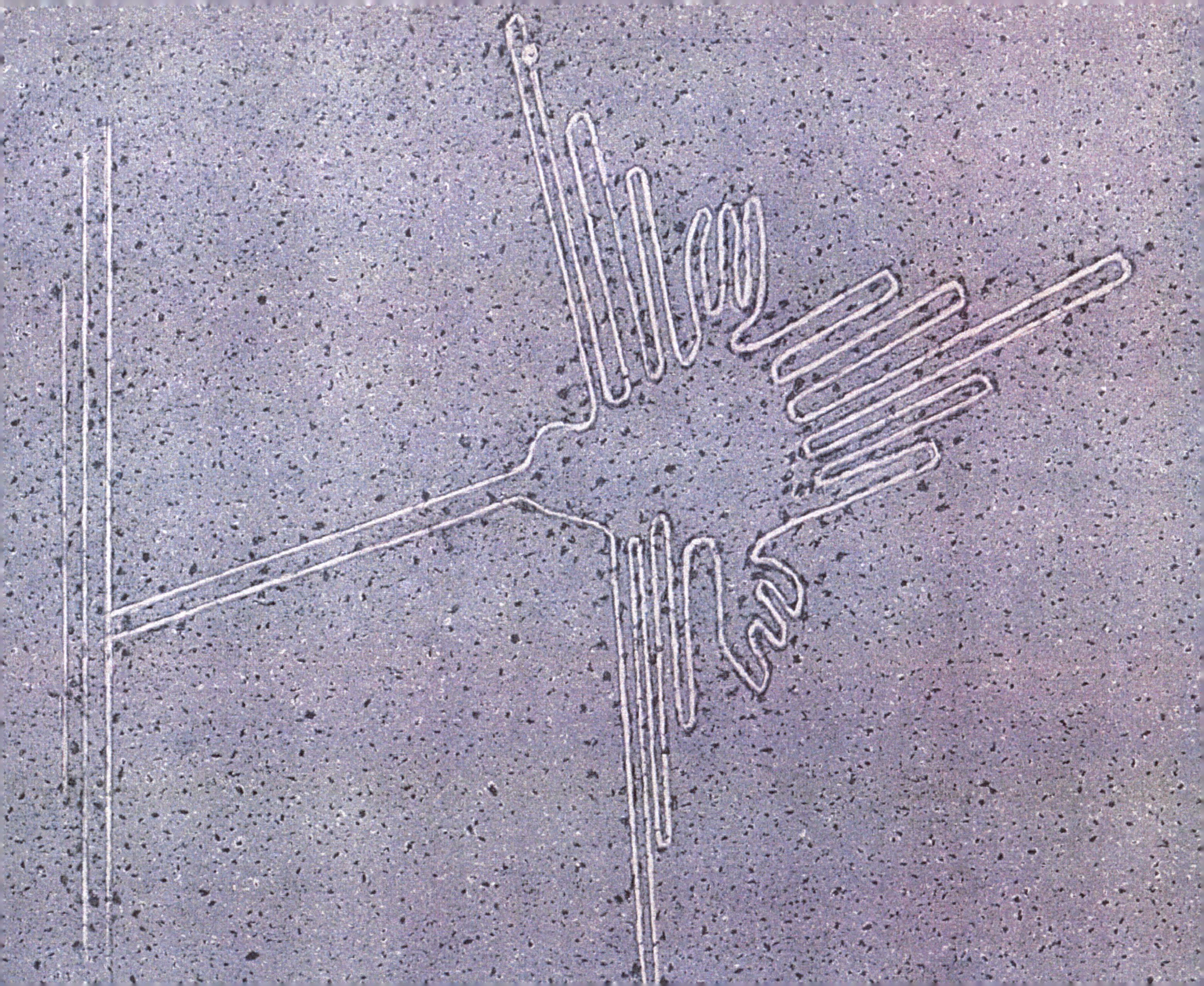

The creatures extend for miles,
all perfectly scaled and drawn.
But why? And for whom?

Maria pondered the answer:
Mystery or magic? Reason or ritual?
Some say even extraterrestrial!

Centuries old, their secret lies safe
beneath the silent stones.

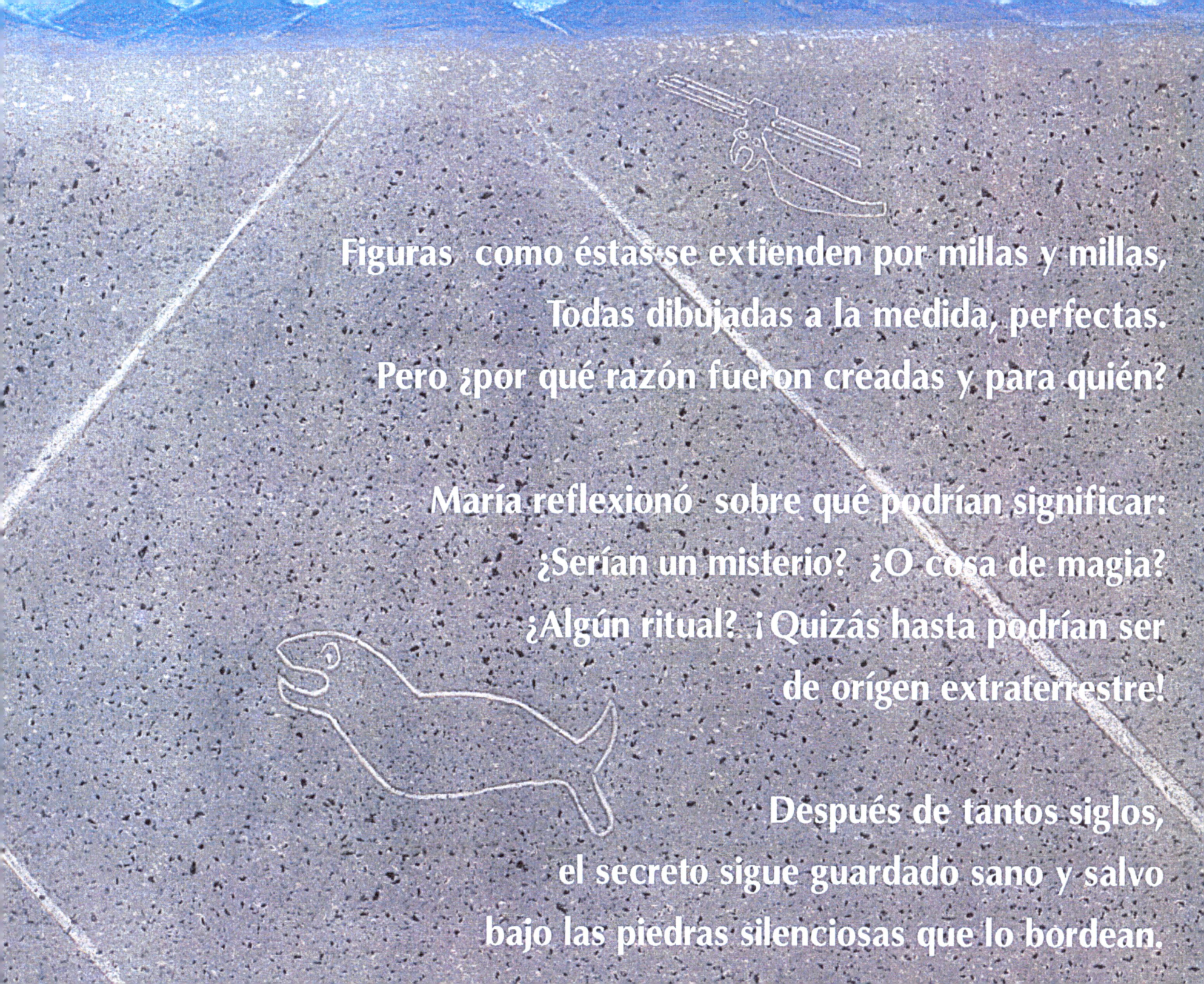

Figuras como éstas se extienden por millas y millas,
Todas dibujadas a la medida, perfectas.
Pero ¿por qué razón fueron creadas y para quién?

María reflexionó sobre qué podrían significar:
¿Serían un misterio? ¿O cosa de magia?
¿Algún ritual? ¡Quizás hasta podrían ser
de orígen extraterrestre!

Después de tantos siglos,
el secreto sigue guardado sano y salvo
bajo las piedras silenciosas que lo bordean.

By day María braved wind and heat,
guarding the beasts of Nazca.

De día María desafía al viento y al calor intenso
Para proteger las criaturas de Nazca.

But when skies would fade to charcoal gray,
she dreamed the ancients' dream:

stones, so white beneath the moon,
they shine bright as stars at night
and reflect an earthly Milky Way
for their gods to take delight.

Dr. Maria Reiche, a German mathematician and geographer working in Peru, wanted to study the Nazca Lines, so in 1946 she moved to the desert there, where she could measure and photograph them. From the Andes mountains, she saw many geometric shapes and huge drawings of animals. She also discovered lines pointing to astrological events, like winter and summer solstice. Other lines pointed to certain stars, like Orion. All these findings led Maria Reiche to regard this 37-mile plain at the foot of the Andes as a gigantic astrological guide that could mark winter and summer solstices so the people would know when it was time to plant and harvest.

Thus, Dr. Reiche believed that some of the lines are solstice markers, and their animal drawings imitate different constellations in the night sky. So because these ancient dwellers also believed that their gods lived high upon the mountains there, their religious leaders probably believed this to be a sacred space. They could have directed the people to construct these figures, lined with rocks with their light undersides turned up so as to shine like stars.

Dr. Reiche continued her work on the Nazca plain until blindness overcame her and her sister came to care for her. In 1994 she received word that Peru's site of the Nazca Lines had been chosen as a World Heritage Site. Four years later Maria Reiche passed away, content that her many years of solitary work would now be shared by a world-wide organization to protect this unique collection of ancient lines so their secrets might continue to be studied by future generations.

Anita Jepson-Gilbert is a poet and teacher who has taught English and ESL classes for many years in Colorado. Her interest in the Nazca Lines led her to read every book she could find about them, and they always referenced the research of Dr. Maria Reiche, a scientist and mathematician living alone on the Nazca desert, measuring and photographing the mysterious Lines. Before Dr. Reiche died in 1998, this author sent her own poem "Maria and the Stars of Nazca," to her, for approval, which Anita soon received. A month later, Reiche's own book, *Mystery on the Desert* arrived, which contains perfect drawings of most of the Nazca images. Thus, all the animal geoglyphs depicted in this book are drawn to scale from Reiche's book.

Then in 2003, this author flew to Peru to visit the Lines herself. She also met with Maria Reiche's closest friends, who could give her more details about Maria's life and her effort to protect the Lines and to have it claimed as a World Heritage Site.

When this bilingual book was first published in 2004 with an English and Spanish audio CD, it received ***1st Prize for Best in Children's Books*** and also ***1st Prize for its Contribution to Literacy*** from the Colorado Independent Publishers Association.

Carmen A. Casis, the translator of this story, is a native of Panama and a long-time resident of Colorado. She is also a Professor Emerita of English and American literature from Regis University in Denver, Colorado, where she taught English for 33 years. She is now retired but is involved in a number of volunteering projects on behalf of civil rights, continuing to offer her translation skills to those in need.

Rodger Osban, this book's illustrator, is a gifted, self-taught artist who has worked in the corporate world as an engineer. Though lacking in formal training, he is a diverse illustrator working in graphite, charcoal, colored pencil, oil, and watercolor. He was selected as one of two illustrator finalists from a pool of 47,000 employees to illustrate a children's book planned for production by the company for which he was employed. His work has been described by critics as *spectacular* and *realistic*.

www.ingramcontent.com/pod-product-compliance
Lightning Source LLC
LaVergne TN
LVHW072306070526
838201LV00099B/286